TEARS OF THE EARTH

Casandra Nightengale

Tears of the Earth

By Casandra Nightengale
© 2020
ISBN: 9798632349352
All rights reserved. No portion of this book may be reproduced (with the exception of brief passages used in reviews) without the written permission of the author. She may be contacted at: casandranightengale@gmail.com

Follow her on Facebook!

All stories in this book are fiction with the exception of <u>Annie's Story</u> which is based on information provided by "Annie" (not her real name) and used by permission.

This book is dedicated to all of those (like the earth) who have shed both tears of joy and those of pain.

TABLE OF CONTENTS

Gaia's Promise
By Casandra Nightengale
© 2015

…And Gaia said to the people assembled before her, "I have brought you forth from a dark place into a future filled with hope. You stand upon a new land as a new people. I have given you guidance that will bring all you desire if you but follow it well. The choice is yours.

'In one thing, however, I give you no quarter. Cherish the children. Raise them in love. Guide them in my ways. Teach them to love and respect the spirit that lives in all things. Admonish them gently, showing them the better path when they error. The children ARE your future. Harm them and you harm me. And in bringing harm, you destroy yourselves. What say you?"

The people, in one accord, lifted up their voices and joyfully proclaimed, "We will!"

How quickly some forgot their vow.

Time spent here

So short, so fleet

Even the earth cries.

Casandra Nightengale
(c) 2014

Pooky
By Casandra Nightengale
© 2015

"Pooky, Mama say we hasta be real quiet. Ain't nobody posed to know we here. I know it cold 'n dark. Here, lay close. Mama say she be back. I know s'been long time. Don' be 'fraid. I rock ya lil bit. Better?" For a moment, the frail five year old crooned tunelessly to her small, one-eyed, tattered bear. As the song faded, she sat the toy up facing her. "Wanna play 'member time? H-m-m. 'Member when Mama brung us a samich? Well, weren't a whole un, but was good! Mama pieced it inna three bits an you give yer bit to me, 'member? You don' never eat, do ya, Pooky, but thas good cuz means ya don' get hungry neither."

Placing her companion over one rail thin shoulder, the girl told the bear, "Don' cry, Pooky, jus' hug up. Mama be back. Be back real soon. Mebbe if'n we sleep a bit, ole hunger bug not bite so hard." Huddled together on the urine stained blanket scrap, they tried to share warmth and drift into the relief of oblivious sleep.

Coward
by Casandra Nightengale
© 2015

Fifteen-year-old Dan Hartman wearily trudged along the winding lane, scuffed leather boots raising small clouds of dust which settled onto his faded trousers. A worn, sweat-soaked shirt clung to his lean torso, the thin fabric straining over broad, sinewy shoulders.

As the ramshackled cabin came into view over the hill, he detoured to the well and splashed cool water from its wooden bucket onto his sweaty face and carefully felt his swollen lip. Looking into the now quiet water, the boy noticed the rips in his shirt and tried not to think of what would happen when he arrived home.

Dan had done his best to avoid the fight but, for some reason, the boys in town would not realize he was no longer the frail, undersized creature they had mercilessly begun to bully over five years ago. Long hours of hard work had transformed that fever-weakened child into the tall, hard-muscled youth whose tanned features reflected from the water. Unable to fight them then, he refused to fight them now.

Four of the boys had joined forces to harass Dan this morning. He had ignored them, but they had persisted, eventually knocking the cornmeal sack from under his arm. When he had stooped to retrieve it, they had attacked him, splitting the sack and spilling its precious contents into the churning dust. Dan's shirt had been torn and his lip bloodied before he had been able to free himself.

Flashing a look of contempt at his tormentors, Dan had sprinted out of town and jogged toward his refuge in the distant hills. Maybe he was a coward, but the boy had vowed to never become like his brawling father.

Finger combing his dark hair into some sort of order, Dan sighed. It was almost sundown. He should have been home long ago.

As the cabin door creaked open, a harsh voice from the dim interior asked, "Zat you, Dan?"

"Yes, Paw."

"Cum 'ere." The boy closed the door and walked over to where Jed Hartman's fleshy, six foot frame was sprawled across a crude wooden chair. A thick crop of grizzled hair poked out from under a battered, sweat-stained Stetson. Cold brown eyes stared from under heavy brows. Dan was relieved to see that the whiskey in the bottle on the knife scarred table was only partially consumed, his father somewhat sober.

"Whar ya bin, boy?"

"In town, Paw…I got my wages an' Mr. Collins wouldn't let us charge no more food, so I paid on the bill," Dan answered hesitantly.

"Yer supposed ta bring thet money straight home!" Jed reminded, his eyes narrowing.

"I know, Paw, but Mr. McCullough needed me ta help load some cattle on the train an'…"

"Whar's the rest?" Jed interrupted, lurching to his feet, the chair tumbling to the floor. The boy slowly backed away before answering.

"There ain't none left, Paw. I got us some cornmeal, but…the sack…got tore. I…I'm sorry," Dan finished in a whisper. He could sense his father's anger building.

"I heered 'bout thet fight," Jed informed coldly. "I also heered ya ran away." Dan swallowed hard. Jed had probably been in the saloon as usual.

"Yer a coward!" Jed accused, closing the distance between them.

"Paw…I…"

"Shet yer sassy mouth!" Jed bellowed, slapping the boy sharply across the face. "Yer a no good, wuthless coward! Ya may be growed like a man, but ya don' act it! When I wuz yer age I cud lick most anybody aroun', but you…you…" Jed paused, too angry for words. Finally he hissed, "Git on out ta the barn. I'll larn ya ta be a man—one way or tuther!"

"Paw, please…no," Dan breathed hoarsely.

"Move!"

Jed jerked Dan out of the cabin and pushed the boy ahead of him, cursing and kicking him when he fell. When they reached the decaying barn, Jed yanked aside the flimsy door and roughly shoved Dan inside the building.

The boy shuddered inwardly as he felt the tattered remains of his shirt being torn away from his body. Now naked to the waist, Dan silently turned toward the outer wall as Jed reached for the whip. There was no escape, no merciful hand to stop his father now that Ma was dead. Bitterly, the boy took a firm grip on the wooden beam in front of him as Jed's voice penetrated the semi-darkness. "Ya stinkin' coward! I'll larn ya not ta run from a fight!"

The plaited leather struck heavily across Dan's back and shoulders. Mutely the boy steeled himself, muscles knotting tightly. Again and again the whip scored his flesh, leaving an ugly lattice of livid welts and bloody furrows. Gritting his teeth, Dan dug his fingernails into the soft wood of the rotting timber. The pain was intense, but crying out would only make things worse. Dan sensed that Jed would not stop this time until his anger had cooled. The boy hoped he could stand the punishment until then. Savagely he blinked away the welling tears, closed his eyes and sucked his breath in sharply. If he could show Paw he could endure this suffering, maybe, just maybe—but, oh, how it hurt! Every fiber cried out in agony! He had been beaten before, but never as brutally as this. "God…please!" he prayed silently. It was a struggle to remain upright, his traitorous body recoiling with every blow. His legs began to tremble as dizziness threatened to send him into unconscious oblivion.

"Had enough—COWARD?

Dan flinched involuntarily as the sound of Jed's voice entered his private hell. It was over. Slowly the boy relaxed his tensed posture and leaned his head against the wall. His breath came in short, hollow gasps.

"Git on out an' do yer chores," Jed spat as he coiled the whip and strode out of the barn.

For a moment Dan just stood there, breathing heavily, trying to swallow the huge lump in his throat. Jed had still called him a coward. Tears blurred the boy's vision as he turned and stumbled toward the door. With a shaky hand, he steadied himself against the wall as another wave of dizziness swept over him. A bitter groan escaped his lips as he slid to the ground and fainted.

It was daylight before Dan awoke and found himself lying face down in his bunk, a pungent salve smeared over his throbbing wounds. Did Jed really care, or was his concern only for the money he would not have if Dan could not return to his job? The problem demanded too much effort to solve, so the boy surrendered to fevered sleep.

Mary McCullough watched as her husband, Angus, sat deep in thought, the man absently swirling a bit of fluffy biscuit in a pool of rich creamy gravy. How she loved her bearded Scottish bear. Crowned with a mane of fiery chestnut, his great height and brawny, muscular build inspired fear in some, but Mary knew that beneath that hairy barrel chest lay the heart of a caring man.

Perhaps she should have waited to voice her concerns. Lord knew that Angus already had enough on his mind having just returned from his trip to the cattle markets. In an effort to lighten the mood, Mary laid her hand on her husband's forearm and teased, "Angus?...Angus, fer pity sake, don' drown the poor thin'!"

"Hm-m-mp? What's that yer sayin', lass?"

"Yer a drowin' yer breakfast, mon."

Suddenly realizing what he was doing, Angus placed the fork across his plate. Turning to his wife, he asked, "Yer sure ye've no seen the lad a' tall since I've bin gone?"

"Nay, Angus, not a glimpse. I dinna mean ta cause ya worry, but 'tis so unlike the laddie to let so much time pass wi'out at least stoppin' by ta sample me cookin'."

"Aye, lass, 'tis what has me worried. He would no take the use of the mare whilest I was gone, aither. Helped me herd the beasties aboard that iron dragon, took his money an' bid me safe journey,---Ye nae think he's gone away, do ye?"

"Perhaps, but 'tis not more likely he's bin helpin' his father?" Mary suggested.

"Ah, lass, wouldst that were true, but I fear not. Their poor place is all run doon. No livestock save a scrawny horse, a few chickens an' a wild, crazy bull. The only work done be done by the laddie. His father seems to care fer naught but his whiskey an' gamblin'. Aye, 'tis said the mon has the very temper o' Lucifer when the drink is upon him. Oft times ha'e I seen Dan bruised, but nary a word does he say agin the mon." Angus shook his head and sighed. "I think 'tis best I ride o'er an' see 'boot the laddie meself."

Seeing the worried look on his wife's face, Angus smoothed her flaxen hair with a calloused hand and gently hugged her to his chest. "Ah Mary…I'll ne'er unnerstan' why the good Lord ne'er blest us wi' wee ones. The way ye fret o'er the laddie, sure He's knowin' ye'd mother well."

For a moment neither spoke. Finally, Mary sniffed and cleared her throat. Pulling slowly from Angus' embrace, she wiped her tears and stared at the floor. "Aye, husband," she agreed huskily, "but 'tis not our place ta question His will…Best ye saddle the horse an' look ta the lad." Without looking back, Mary walked into the kitchen.

His own vision still hazy, Angus turned to the window, "Mary!" he shouted, recognizing the figure that had entered their lane, "Ye best make more breakfast. The laddie's cum!" Hearing her joyful reply, Angus left the house. He had not told his wife the boy was limping.

Seeing Angus hurrying toward him, Dan greeted, "Mornin', Sir. Sorry I'm late."

"Late! I'll say yer late, laddie! Ye've had Mary all a'worry when ye no came whilest I was gone," Angus scolded teasingly, but something in Dan's expression made him stop. "I nay be upset wi' ye lad," he added. "Ha' ye eaten yet?"

"No, Sir, but…I'm not very hungry."

"Not hungry? Och, now. Ha' ye been ill? Ye do look a bit fevered," Angus asked with concern.

"Yes, Sir. I caught sick fer a spell," Dan lied regretfully. It would do no good to reveal the real reason.

"Well, Mary's got just the thin' ta tempt ye now—a plate o' her feather light biscuits with gravy. Best we no keep her waitin', eh?" Dan reluctantly agreed.

Watching the boy's feeble effort to eat confirmed Angus' belief that something was wrong. Dan's usually bright, clear eyes were dull and lifeless, his high-boned cheeks colored with an unnatural flush. Unable to force any more of the delicious food into his unstable stomach, the boy thanked his hostess and rose from the table. Angus followed him into the yard.

"Ye're sure ye feel up ta workin' today, lad?"

"I'll be fine, Sir," the boy lied again. He had not felt strong enough to return to work, but Jed had threatened him with another beating if he did not go.

"Aye, if ye say so.—Well—we be needin' ta fence a small pasture fer the new calves. I know yer a wonder at splittin' rails, laddie, but I was thinkin' on usin' the barbed wire. Nasty stuff 'tis sure, but 'twill save time. How say ye, Dan?" The boy nodded.

As the day grew hotter, Dan's dizzy spells returned. Seeing the boy was faltering, Angus called a halt and headed toward a shady spot on the stream bank nearby. While the big man settled beneath a tree, Dan carefully lowered himself to his stomach and drank deeply from the cool water, his body hugging the damp earth.

"Och, lad, the sun's a demon today. Feels good ta take a breather," Angus declared, extending his legs and crossing his arms over his chest. Dan knew they had stopped because of him and was grateful.

"Thanks, Sir."

"Angus, laddie. How oft do I ha' ta remind ye? Call me Angus."

"Angus," the boy repeated dutifully as he rested his chin on his folded arms and stared across the water. Why couldn't Paw be more like Angus, he wondered?

Dan was lost in thought moments later when his employer asked, "Are ye ready ta tackle that fence agin, laddie?" Yawning, the boy absently answered, "Aye," and was startled by a roar of laughter.

"We'll make a Scot out o' ye yet, lad."

Dan was mechanically going through the motions of tacking the wire into place when dizziness again stabbed at him and he fell.

"Are ye a'right?" Angus asked, running to his side.

"I…I dunno…I think so." The boy sat up and put a hand to his aching head.

"Och, lad, let me see yer arm!"

Afraid one of the whip welts had reopened, Dan glanced at his shoulder. The shirt was freshly torn, the flesh seeping blood.

"Barbed wire makes a nasty cut, lad. I'd best git ye to the house an' fix it."

"But Sir, it's only a scratch!" Dan protested, covering the wound with his hand.

"Aye, but an awfully deep scratch," the rancher countered.

Silently Dan allowed himself to be ushered to the house. He wanted to run and hide, but he hurt too badly to do more than place one foot in front of the other.

Once inside the kitchen, the boy was seated on a stool and the necessary supplies placed on the table next to him.

"Ye best take off yer shirt, Dan," Angus suggested. When the boy hesitated, McCullough glanced at his wife and added gently, "Dunna be shy. Mary will no be offended."

"Please, Sir. It don' need no doctorin'," Dan plead, a look of desperation in his dark eyes.

"Dan," Angus said firmly. Reluctantly, the boy unfastened the laces and allowed the garment to be removed. There was a shocked silence as the rancher and his wife stared in disbelief at the maze of infected wounds that covered the boy's naked flesh.

"Who did this, lad?" Angus asked softly. The boy did not answer. "Yer father?"

Dan stared at the floor. Without raising his eyes, he hoarsely whispered, "Yes, Sir."

Mary looked at her husband in despair and then busied herself heating some water so the boy would not see her tears. Angus knelt in front of Dan and gently raised the boy's trembling chin. "Why, lad?" The boy remained silent. "Was he drunk agin?"

Shuddering with memory, Dan closed his eyes and stammered, "N-no. N-not real drunk."

"Then, why?"

Hesitantly the story came forth. When Dan finished, he anxiously looked into the pale blue of McCullough's eyes and haltingly asked, "Am I…am I a…coward, Angus?" The murderous anger the Scotsman felt toward Jed Hartman was suddenly replaced by compassion for this boy who almost fearfully awaited his answer.

"Nay, lad. Yer no coward." Seeing the relief that flooded Dan's face, Angus continued.

"There may cum a time when ye fight fer sumthin' ye truly wish ta defend, but ye dinna ha' ta be a bully ta prove yer a mon. Many's the time I've walked away from someun who's only lookin' fer a fight. There be no shame in that, Dan. Yer father canna unnerstan' this an' his drinkin' dinna help." He paused, noticing the boy was shivering. "Och, we better clean ye up a bit. Cum in an' lie doon on the sofa."

While Mary carefully cleansed the fevered wounds, Angus warmed some milk and liberally laced it with laudanum and honey. After Dan had been bandaged, Angus supported the boy while he drained the cup and lowered him again to the soft cushions. The potion took effect and Dan slipped into drugged slumber.

"He'll be oot fer quite a while, Mary, but 'twill be fer the best." Looking again at the bandaged form, Angus turned away and slammed one massive fist into the palm of the other hand. "God Almighty, I dunna see how a mon could flog his own son…an' all because he wunna fight! I've a mind ta give Jed Hartman a thrashin' he'll long remember!"

"Nay, Angus," Mary chided softly as she wiped Dan's face with a cool damp cloth. "'Twould solve naught an' ye know it." Realizing that his wife was right, Angus let his hands fall to his sides.

"Aye, 'twould only cause more trouble fer the lad." Shaking his head, he left the house and resumed his work.

When the last of the wire was in place, Angus returned. Mary met him at the kitchen door. "Dan's still asleep," she whispered.

"Aye. I suppose I'd best go tell Hartman where the laddie is. I doubt that he cares, but I dunna what more trouble fer Dan."

"I'll stay wi' the lad 'til his fever breaks," Mary offered. Pausing, she added, Angus…take care that ye do naught rashly."

"Dunna fret, lass. I'll be home a bit after sundoon." He brushed her cheek with a light kiss and left.

The black gelding covered the distance much faster than it had taken the boy to do so earlier in the day. Upon arrival, Angus tethered his mount and knocked on the cabin door.

Receiving no answer, the rancher cautiously looked inside. The stench of sweat and liquor in the empty room was overpowering. Closing the door, McCullough strode purposefully toward the barn. Finding it, too, deserted, he started to leave when a plaited coil looped over a wooden peg caught his eye. Stepping closer, Angus saw the bloodstains and was suddenly filled with anger. How could Hartman be cruel enough to use that whip on his own son? No wonder the boy limped; it was amazing he could walk at all!

Grabbing the whip Angus stormed out of the barn. Slinging the offending coil over his saddle horn, the Scot returned to the cabin, hastily wrote a note and threw it on the table. He then left, unaware that Jed Hartman could neither read nor write.

Tender care and nourishing food over the next few days sped Dan's recovery. The boy, however, seemed frustrated at being confined to the house. In an effort to make him feel useful,

Mary no had Dan busily paring apples for the
evening's dessert.

Outside, the wind fiercely stirred the soil
into a dirty haze. Storm clouds gathered and
rain began to fall, slowly at first and then in a
wild deluge that rushed to soothe the parched
earth.

Mary had just served the hot apple
dumplings with sweet cream when the sound of
rapid hoof beats was heard above the storm.
She sent a questioning look toward Angus who
shrugged. Motioning for her and Dan to
continue eating, the rancher stood up and went
to the front door.

Jed Hartman jerked his lathered horse to a
sliding stop as Angus stepped out onto the
covered porch, rifle in hand.

"Whar's Dan?" the drunken man
demanded. "H'I…know he's ahidin'
some'her's on this high-fangled ranch o' yourn.
He…he cain't h'run 'way from me h'an git
'way wif h'it!"

"The laddie's here, Hartman. He's been
too sick to travel," Angus explained evenly.

"Sick? Huh! 'e's a lazy no good…thet's wha' 'e h'is! Whar h'is 'e? I'll larn 'im not ta run 'way from 'is paw!"

"Like ye 'larned' him not ta run from a fight?"

"Wha'?"

"It's a wunner the lad's alive after the way he beat him! What's the matter wi' ye, mon? The lad o' yourn works 'is heart out an' whadda ye do, ye lazy drunken sot? Ye use his money fer yer own pleasures an' then flog the laddie senseless because he wunna be a bully like ye! It takes a real mon ta walk away from a fight, Hartman—a real mon!"

"Why h'you…," Jed snarled. "Whar's thet loudmouthed kid o' mine? Ah'll fix 'im fer tellin' lies!...An' you…ya lousy furiner…yer gonna pay fer meddlin'," Hartman threatened, drawing a hunting knife from his boot.

Trusting that the drunken man could not be accurate at the distance which separated them, the Scot challenged boldly, "Go ahead, mon—throw it! Give me a good reason ta drag ye off that bony nag an' give ye a taste o' the lash yer so fond o' usin' on Dan!"

Seeing the determined look in those icy eyes and the massive hand clenching the rifle, Jed yanked his skinny sorrel around, dug his spurs into its flanks and galloped it down the muddy lane, cursing all the way. As McCullough watched Dan's father disappear into the driving rain, he heard the door open. Mary stepped out onto the porch.

"Ye took an awful chance, Angus."

"Aye, but he was nae gunna hurt the laddie whilest I was here…How is Dan?"

"A bit shaken, but more worried aboot our safety…He's a good lad, husband. Be there no way we kin keep him here? He'll cum ta no good wi' that father o' his."

"I dunna know, Mary. Perhaps. Let's ha' a talk wi' him." Together they entered the house.

"Dan, lad, will ye cum here a moment?" Angus called. There was no response except for the renewed fury of the storm. Leaving her husband to search the rest of the house, Mary went into the kitchen to clean up the meal. The back door was open. "Angus! Angus, he's gone!"

Rain continued its relentless downpour, heedless of the youth slogging his way across the sodden countryside. With dogged determination, Dan made his way to the small grove of trees at his journey's end. Heartsick and exhausted, he sank to the ground, pillowed his head in his arms and cried until the tears would come no more.

Cold rain and warm salty tears combined in a rivulet that followed the grooves on the crude maker. The boy did not need to read the inscription. He knew what it said—SARAH HARTMAN. He had spent many hours painstakingly carving those few letters in final tribute to Ma. Why did she have to die? She had been so very much like Mary—small, blond, fair. Ma had been the only bright spot in his early years. He could still remember her gentle patience while teaching him his "useless lessons" as Paw had called them. A disapproving look from her and always hurt

much more than Paw's spankings. Oh, yes—
they had been spankings then! Ma had always
managed to stop him before they had become
any worse. Paw had accused her of coddling
him, had said a good thrashing would make a
man out of him. But, somehow, Paw could not
argue with that quiet look of hers.

Yes, those had been good days. Luck,
however, had failed them. Paw's gambling had
lost their land, forcing them to become despised
squatters on this small farm. Then the fever had
come. It had killed Ma and had left him a
hollow shadow of the once robust child he had
been. Maybe it would have been better if he had
died instead.

After Ma's death, Paw's drinking and
temper had become worse. Caring nothing now
for their home, he had allowed it to fall into
ruin, spending most of his time either gambling
or in a drunken stupor. Paw's only pride
seemed to be a bull he had won during a rare
lucky gambling streak. A mean and surly
creature, it seemed to be a fitting companion for
its owner.

The storm finally spent itself, allowing a full moon to shine from beyond empty clouds. The boy lay quietly now, listening to the soothing night sounds. All seemed peaceful and at rest in his secluded haven. How good it would be to simply stay here forever.

It was almost midnight when Dan returned home. The odor of liquor wafted from the tiny window. Shaking his head, he opened the door and slipped inside the cabin. There was a sudden movement in the darkness, a flash of moonlight on metal. Conditioned reflexes made the boy duck. The knife barely missed him and buried itself into the wood where his head had been. A string of profanity followed as the drunken man lunged forward.

"Paw! It's me—Dan!"

The boy stepped back and fumbled for the door latch. Before he could reach it, however, the back of Jed's clenched fist cracked across his ear. Dan dodged his tormentor and ignored the verbal tirade until ill reference was made to his mother. Greatly angered, the boy swung at his father, his fist connecting with an open jaw.

Spitting blood, Jed bellowed, "Sassy whelp! I'll larn ya not ta hit yer ole man!"

"Thet's what ya've bin wantin' me ta do, ain't it? Ya've bin wantin' me ta fight! Wal, ya ain't gonna drag Ma's name through the mud an' git away with it! She was a good woman— too good fer the likes o' you! Yer nuthin' but a drunken bully! You ain't no good ta nobody! Why didn't you die instead?" seethed Dan, fists clenched, heart racing wildly. Never before had he stood up to his father and his stomach crawled with fear of the consequences. Come what may, however, he had said his piece.

Jed was quite surprised, even in his drunken state, but was not about to back down to his son. "Think ya kin whip yer ole man, cub? Wal…common an' try!"

"I ain't got no more quarrel with ya, Paw. Jist leave Ma outta it," the boy replied, slowly lowering his fists.

"Aw…naw!..Ya ain't gonna back out this time!"

Dan turned away, walked over and sat on the edge of his bunk. "I ain't gonna fight ya, Paw," he answered quietly.

"COWARD!" Jed shrieked, grabbing the empty whiskey bottle and hurling it at his son. The boy ducked and the bottle shattered against the wall.

"Stop it, Paw!" Dan said in disgust. "Yer drunk! Please…just go ta bed."

"Drunk h'am I? I'll show ya how drunk h'I am!"

As Jed pulled the thick leather belt from around his waist, Dan bolted toward the door only to be grabbed by the hair and hurled back into the room. "Not this time, boy," Jed snarled as he hit Dan across the face with the metal buckle. Dazed, the boy stumbled backward, tripped and fell, his head striking the wall. In a fit of drunken fury, Jed beat his son, cursing all the while. So set on revenge was he that he did not even realize Dan was beyond feeling.

Day dawned to a brief rain squall. Inside the cabin, Dan awoke, slowly raised himself on one elbow and looked across the dimly lit room.

Jed was stretched across a bunk, deep in drunken slumber; the belt lay limply beneath his open fist. The boy shuddered and mouthed an unvoiced cry of anguish as he sank back down to the rough floor. Paw would never understand, would never accept him as he was, so why try? The boy drifted into fitful sleep filled with unpleasant dreams.

When Dan again awoke, the rain had stopped and the burning rays of the sun now reached through the window. Stiffly he arose, noticed his father still slept and quietly left the cabin. It would be better for him if the chores were done when Jed awoke.

Heat and humidity added to Dan's discomfort as he toiled at his tasks. He could tell Jed was now awake by the smoke coming from the chimney. "Probably brewin' coffee fer his hangover," the boy mused bitterly as he limped across the pasture to catch the horse. Discovering that the poor animal had not fared well with Jed the night before, Dan took time to gently tend its wounds. The bull could be fed later.

Jed Hartman sat slumped over the table, staring at the dying flames in the fireplace. He had had another blackout last night and was almost afraid to remember. Dried blood on his belt spoke of violence—violence most likely done to Dan. He did not really hate his son. The boy was just too much like Sarah. That quiet strength was something Jed both hated and envied. His son was no coward, but he would never admit this to the boy.

Suddenly, Jed became aware that someone was riding toward the cabin. He squinted into the sunlight through the open door as a mud spattered black gelding splashed into view. Seeing Angus, Jed spat on the floor and lumbered outside the cabin. "Whaddya want?"

Glancing at Jed's disheveled appearance, McCullough replied, "Where's Dan?"

"Why?"

"I want ta speak wi' the laddie, Hartman," Angus replied firmly as he dismounted. Seeing that his visitor was determined to stay, Jed ordered,

"Stay here. I'll find 'im."

Noticing the boy in the fenced pasture nearby, Jed sullenly trudged across the yard and through the muddy corral. Sliding through the gate, he yelled, "Dan!" Getting the boy's attention, Jed took a few steps into the barnyard, waving his arms and gesturing toward the cabin.

Dan released the horse and started toward his father when a dark shadow caught his eye. The bull! Last night's storm must have freed him from his pen! With an angry squeal, the beast charged toward Jed.

"Paw!" Dan shouted. "Git outta there— the bull's loose!"

Ignoring his own injuries, the boy scaled the pasture fence and sprinted across the slick ground. He must attract the animal's attention, but how? His shirt! Wincing, Dan ripped the frayed garment from his back and began to wave it violently. "Hey there! Hey, ya stupid bull—over here! Run, Paw!"

Terror rooted Jed to the ground. Only the animal's temporary confusion at having two targets gave Dan the necessary time to reach his father and knock him aside as the beast rushed past. The boy grimaced as a searing fire shot up his thigh. One of the bull's horns had sliced his leg in passing. Shoving Jed toward the corral, Dan grabbed his shirt and dodged as the beast whirled and charged. Jed hastily climbed the gate and was met by Angus. The Scot was carrying a rifle.

"Gimme thet gun!" Jed cried, grabbing the weapon. Turning Hartman saw Dan's injured leg collapse. The boy fell. The bull stood over him. Jed fired, but missed the animal's vital area in fear of hitting his son. The creature bellowed as the bullet entered its muscular shoulder. Dan tried to roll free, but the animal suddenly lunged, head down. One of those huge horns impaled the boy and the bull flung him up and over his head, slamming Dan to the muddy ground behind him. Jed blinked hot tears from his eyes, took sharp aim and fired. The maddened beast screamed and turned to attack the corral, but the bullet had found its mark. With a low grunt, the bull collapsed.

Throwing the rifle to McCullough, Jed ran to his son's side. Kneeling in the trampled sod, he carefully rolled the prostrate form onto its back and cradled the head in his arms. Blood flowed from the gaping would in Dan's side. In desperation, Jed wadded the torn shirt and pressed it into the crimson gash.

Angus now knelt next to him. Their differences set aside, the two men did all they could to stop the bleeding. Nothing helped—the wound was too deep. Dan suddenly moaned and arched his back in pain. "Easy, laddie…easy," Angus soothed, gripping the boy's hand tightly. Gently, he stroked Dan's sweaty brow until the spasm passed. Glancing toward the boy's father, McCullough saw the overwhelming grief in the man's eyes. Why did some people never appreciate what they had until it was too late? Reluctant to leave, Angus still sensed that Jed wished to be alone with his son. Squeezing Dan's hand one last time, the Scot stood slowly to his feet and walked toward the blurry figure of his horse.

Tears streamed unchecked down Jed Hartman's face. There was so little time, but the words he needed to say were still locked within him, struggling to escape. Looking down at the ashen face, Jed finally spoke, his voice cracked and hoarse. "Ya done a brave thing, Dan. A real…brave…thing.–I'm proud…awful proud o' ya…son." The boy's eyes slowly opened. For a brief moment he held Jed's gaze, understanding passing between them before he slipped into eternity.

Jed carefully lowered his son's body to the ground. Tears blinded the man; his body trembled. Struggling to his feet, Jed shook his fist at the cloudless sky. "WHY?" he cried in anguish. As that cry echoed across the prairie, his conscience answered, "COWARD!"

Annie's Story
(written by Casandra Nightengale based on information given to her by "Annie")

"We don't have the money to spend on knick-knacks. If you can find a broken horse, maybe someone will give it to you," my father says. My young inner self hears, "You aren't worth the price of a whole, undamaged china horse. You are only worth the free, discarded, broken ones." My inner translator stamps on my brain, "You are only worth what no one else wants. You are not worthy of great stuff. You are lucky to get leftovers."

"You've been bad—no ice cream for you! You are WRONG—go to your room and don't come out until you say you're WRONG!" my father orders. (*But I'm NOT wrong.*)

"U-m-m-m-! We're having ice cream and you can have it if you say you're WRONG!" (*That would be a lie—I'm not wrong.*)

"SAY YOU'RE WRONG!"

(*I don't get ice cream very often—but saying I'm wrong would make me a liar. I did no wrong. So I sit in a dark room listening to my family eating ice cream—and I cry.)*

Born to a controlling fundamentalist minister father and a cowed and submissive mother, my young life was one of near poverty and abuse. My father ruled us totally. He decided what kinds of used clothes we could take from the missionary barrel to wear (we rarely had new ones), what hairstyle we were allowed, what books we read. And so on. He ate the best and his fill of what food we had and his will was ours (or it had better be if you wanted to avoid a beating with the thick leather belt he hung in the closet.)

At a young age, I saw discrepancies in bible teachings, but when I questioned them, I was "of the devil" and was beaten. I was also "cursed" with intuition and an ability to see spirits, but learned to keep that quiet for survival sake.

Although I was the first grandchild on either side of the family, I was a girl. When my brother was born, I was "discarded" emotionally and ignored in favor of the blessed male. He was what mattered, not a mere female, so I tried throughout my life to be better, faster, and smarter than the male population so I could receive some sort of recognition.

When the sexual abuse started, I also longed unconsciously to be male. Maybe "he" (my father) wouldn't do those things if I was a boy. I began to gain weight in an unconscious attempt to become unattractive. Men don't like fat women—at least he didn't. If he didn't like me, maybe he would leave me alone. No such luck—the abuse continued. If I did not submit, he would do it to my younger sister, he said. I was already "damaged goods". Maybe I could save her. Later I discovered I had not. He had abused her as well, although not as severely. He also later abused my nieces and had made attempts on at least one woman in the church during a counseling session. When confronted by the church elders concerning the woman who came forward and accused him, my father convinced them she was having fantasies about him and her whole family was expelled from the church. To the outer world, he presented the façade of a caring man of god. Only our family saw his true self.

My mother died when I was twenty and my father remarried. My siblings grew, married and started lives of their own. I began to quietly follow my own spiritual path and embrace my "other world" gifts. My abilities were rarely revealed to any one and never to my family. I studied many religions and spiritual teachings in an effort to understand what my soul sought and what I truly believed. I shared the results with few. Afraid—my inner child was still afraid.

Years passed and I continued working, peeling away at the onion layers of my life—but it was going so very slowly. Early conditioning was hard to overcome.

One example was tithing which was drilled into me almost from birth. One tenth (plus offering) belonged to god—even if you had little to eat. I remember finding a dime when I was five. For that meager amount I could purchase a large helium filled balloon. I had seen them but had never owned one. I begged my father to take me to the store so I could buy one. He reminded me that one cent of that dime belonged to god and if I did not give it to god, I was a thief. (*But if I gave god a penny, I would not have enough for my balloon!)* My father took me to the store, all the time laying a massive guilt trip on my five-year-old self. We stood in line to get the balloon. When it was my turn, he again reminded me of my obligation to heaven. Crying, I gave in and we went home—without a balloon.

Thinking back on this incident as an adult, I realized that god did not need my money. It was just another way to control my life. With this realization, my abundance issues began to fade away.

During meditation one day, I was "told" to buy back my freedom. *WHAT?* As a symbolic gesture of claiming my total independence, I was to take a penny, bury it in the ground next to a tall, strong tree and verbally declare myself free. I did that the next day. That night I had strange dreams, but awakened feeling as if bands of steel had been removed from my chest. I WAS worthy of having good in my life! I mattered! It was okay to be different. My throat lost its tightness and I could now breathe deeper.

"If it harms no one—including yourself—do as you will" is now my life guide. A walk in nature is my church service as I am now spiritual but not religious. Fears and insecurities from the past still crop up from time to time, but thankfully, I am now free to be a new me.

*Some are crying tears
of joy*

Others tears of pain--

*Come my darling, don't
be shy*

*Join spirits dancing in
the rain!*

*Casandra Nightengale
(c) 2014*

Star Child

By Casandra Nightengale
© 2015

Maddie left me far too soon. Her father left us before she was born, claiming he was too young and had too much world to see to be tied down with a kid. We divorced and I carried and birthed her alone.

People would have thought me crazy if I had told them that my child and I communicated before she was born. I could hear her thoughts in my head and she would kick and wiggle when she thought something was humorous. She told me she was a girl long before the sonogram confirmed it and also said her name would be Madison Renee.

Maddie entered life on a dark night filled with stars. It seemed as if she was anxious to begin her journey. My labor was short and soon this precious life was placed in my arms, wrapped in a pink blanket. Tracing a finger gently across her rosebud lips, I murmured to her, "Welcome to Earth my precious angel." Her eyes opened and I swear she smiled.

Life was interesting with Maddie around. She continued her mental communication with me until she was able to verbalize and was always alert and interested in her surroundings.

"What are you doing?" she mentally asked one day when I moved her crib into my home office.

"Writing," I answered.

"Why do you write?"

"I write because I enjoy it and to make money so we can live." She thought a moment and then cooed and giggled in a baby sort of way.

"What?" I asked.

"Earth ways are so different from star ways," she replied, rolling onto her side so she could more easily observe me.

"Care to explain?"

Maddie told me that in the star place, life is peace and harmony. No one is greedy or above anyone else. Everyone does what brings them joy, so what they do is not a job. There is no money. Everyone's needs are met and there is no hunger or want. The beings pour love into their creations and no product is valued more than another. Fine jewelry is no more sought after than a beautiful blanket created by another.

If someone tires of one sort of "work", they train for another. There is no competition or jealousy in the professions and if you prefer to just meditate in the gardens that day instead of creating, it is acceptable.

If I had not been used to my daughter's mental dialogs by now, this may have been a bit fanciful. She was convinced that she came from a place in the stars and I was not going to disabuse that notion.

As Maddie grew older, I would ask her about the star place. Sometimes she would answer briefly, but usually she would laugh and tell me to enjoy today. My daughter lived in the moment, whether that involved chasing a firefly or sitting quietly and watching ants bring food into their nest.

She smiled at my concept of God and told me that the creator was not some old guy with a beard sitting on a cloud waiting to punish us for whatever sins we did. When questioned as to her beliefs, she simply referred to the creator of all as the One and said we are all one. Religion separates us, spirituality unites. So, I released my childhood religion with all of its confining rules and embraced the spiritual idea of the One. It made more sense.

Maddie's foray into public education was a fiasco. She could not tolerate the mental conditioning and dogma of the regimented curriculum and was often frustrated when the teachers ignored or made light of her questions.

Never one to act out, Maddie came home one day and announced that she was not going back. It was a waste of her time. I had to agree and made arrangements to home school her. She absorbed the required information quickly and that left her with plenty of time to explore in the woods behind our home or to read or sit in meditation, something she did a lot.

I was busy writing when the doorbell rang. Maddie had ridden her bike into town to return some books to the library and I wasn't expecting her back for at least another hour. Why would she ring the bell? The door was seldom locked and she had a key. Hitting SAVE, I went to the door.

A uniformed officer explained that there had been an accident. A speeding drunk driver had swerved wide coming around a curve on the mountain road and had hit my ten-year-old daughter. She had been rushed to the hospital in critical condition.

Frantically, I grabbed my keys and followed the sirens and lights. All the way there, I tried to get her to answer me on our special mental channel, but there was nothing.

Seeing my child hooked up to monitors and IVs was not as frightening as the continued mental silence. Carefully, I took her hand in mine.

"Maddie. Maddie, I love you. Talk to me, sweetheart." I tried again, reaching for her in my soul. The slender hand twitched and a distant mental voice responded.

"I love you, Mom. The stars are calling and I have to go."

"Why?"

"It's time."

"No!" I wailed in protest, leaning over the inert form and caressing her cheek.

"Remember to make me stardust, Mom. I love you."

The channel went silent and I knew it would not reopen. As the monitors screamed their monotone message, I hugged Maddie and murmured, "Safe journey, my love."

As per her request, Madison was cremated. We had talked about it a couple times and she was adamant that she be returned to stardust and released into the winds. I fulfilled her request and she was scattered, except for a small portion which was sealed into a heart shaped locket that never left my neck.

Time passed and I could not recover from her sudden death. I lost interest in life. Mail piled up, publishers called as deadlines passed. I barely ate and cried a lot. Friends suggested grief counseling, but when I went, it seemed like meaningless platitudes and plastic smiles. The silence in my head was deafening.

I began to meditate. Yes, I had done that with Maddie, but not in as serious a mind as I now possessed. My thoughts drifted again. "Live in the now." What did that mean? It had all seemed so clear when my daughter explained it, but now, I was lost. I called on the creator, the One, for help.

Expecting another sleepless night, I went to bed and fell into a deep slumber. In the velvet vastness of space, the darkness was filled with millions of stars. I floated among them. Stillness filled me. Maddie loved the stars and if what she believed was true, she was out here somewhere among them. I missed her so much. Her sudden death gave me no time to prepare for the separation. What was I to do?

"Come to Peru," a mental voice suggested. It was male and much older.

"What?"

"Come to us in the sacred ruins of Machu Picchu. You will find what you seek."

Here I saw the wizened and leathery face of what appeared to be a tribal shaman.

"Just go to Machu Picchu? How will I find you? What do I do?"

His image smiled at me. *"Trust the One and come."* The image faded and suddenly I was awake.

Trust and come. Well, weirder things had happened in my life. I showered, got on the internet and made travel plans.

After a grueling climb, I now stood and looked over the ruins of an ancient complex that sprawled forever. I had seen photos, but being here in person, I could almost feel the history. Slipping a bottle of water from my backpack, I took a long drink, enjoying the wetness on my parched throat. Untying my bandana, I wiped the sweat dripping from my face. Turning once again to the path, I saw him—the shaman from my dream.

"Come." Was all he said before disappearing off of the path and into dense foliage? No one else was in sight.

"Trust in the One," I muttered and walked towards where he had disappeared. A dense fog descended, and I could barely see my guide as he lead me to a destination known only to him.

When the fog cleared, we were standing in a small clearing. In front of us was the opening to a cave. Next to that was a waterfall cascading into a steaming pool. My guide entered the cave and paused just beyond the entrance. I followed. Turning to me he mentally asked, *"Do you believe your daughter lives?"*

"What do you mean? Now?"

"Does SHE live?"

"Her spirit lives. Her body is no more," I replied, clutching my locket. The old man smiled as he closed his eyes and seemed to be communing with someone. With a nod and a sigh, he opened his eyes, took my hands and said aloud, "It is enough."

"What does that mean?" I asked.

Without answering, the shaman led me deeper into the cave and seated me on the rocky floor. Then he built a fire. Squatting on the ground, he began to chant.

Five native women ranging from young to old, walked into the cave. Taking me by the hand, they led me to the pool by the waterfall. Gently they removed my hair from its ponytail and let it fall around my shoulders. Motioning that I should disrobe, I did so, my sweat soaked clothing falling in a pile on the damp ground. They pointed to the pool and I entered, expecting the water to be cold. It was delightfully warm. Taking the pot of unguent I was handed, I bathed. As the sweat left my body and hair, a peace began to descend. Submerging myself to rinse, I felt as if I could stay underwater without the need to breathe—as if the pool was one with my body. It was wondrous.

When I surfaced, the women beckoned, and I left the pool. Gently they patted me dry with a cloth and dressed me in a finely woven robe decorated with beads and tiny brass bells. My hair was combed with a carved jade comb and I was once again led inside the cave. Two woven grass mats now lay on the rocky floor.

As I sat on one mat, four of the women joined the shaman. The other motioned for me to give her Maddie's locket.

"NO!" I protested. "It's all I have left of her." In my mind I heard, *"Believe."* Reluctantly, I gave her the piece. She placed it on the mat next to me and joined the others in a circle that now surrounded me.

All of them began to chant. The verbal language was nothing I could understand, but in my mind, I heard their call. *"Star child. Your earthly mother mourns. She grieves deeply and can find no joy in her life. She has great need of comfort. Hear us."*

Outside the cave, the sun went down. The chanting song went on and on, the tones hauntingly beautiful as it surrounded me, filled me. Stars appeared on the ceiling of the cave and the mat next to me began to glow. Maddie's locket began to fade and was replaced by a form that gradually took shape.

I held my breath and watched as the form became my daughter, also dressed in a woven robe. Hers was of white silver with a sash of cobalt. Bands of woven gold encased her ankles. Wrists donned bracelets of intricate design set with unknown gemstones. My locket lay around her neck. How could this be?

The chanting ceased and the shaman walked to Maddie and touched her lightly on the shoulder. Gesturing towards me, he nodded.

"Mom?"

"Is she real?" I asked the old man.

"As real as you and me," he replied.

"May I touch her?" I asked hopefully.

Grinning a toothless smile, he answered, "Of course."

"Maddie, baby," I murmured as I enveloped my child in a hug. An ocean of tears released and I sobbed uncontrollably. "How can this be? How will I explain her return? Oh, who cares? She's here and we have so much more living to do!"

The shaman put a hand lightly on my shoulder and I heard the mind speak again. *"She is only here for three days. After that she will return to the stars. Enjoy your time together."*

I began to protest and then stopped, realizing that this was a gift. *"Thank you."*

For three days we swam, ate fruit we gathered from the trees near the clearing and talked. I once again enjoyed braiding her hair and we talked some more.

"So, what do you do in the star land my love?" I asked her on the third day.

Maddie peeled a piece of fruit and took a
bite. Juice trickled down her chin. I reached
over and wiped it with the tip of my finger. She
smiled. "I'm studying jewelry making right
now. I can forge gold, silver and electrum and
make stuff like these," she stated pointing to her
jewelry. "Anything I don't keep and wear is
placed in the communal store for anyone to take
and wear. When they tire of it and want
something different, they return the pieces and
select something else." Seeing the look of pride
on my face, she added, "My jewelry work is no
more important than a pastry or loaf of bread
created by the baker. We both pour love into our
creations and it gives us joy."

Tears sprang into my eyes.

"Don't be sad. Mom! I'm fine. I may live
in another place, but I'm still your Madison.
Remember me alive." Reaching up, she
unclasped the locket containing a few of her
ashes. Closing her hand around it, she took a
deep breath. When she opened her hand, the
piece had been transformed into a tasteful
pendant made of gold. Small diamonds gave the
look of stars, but in no constellation I could
recognize. Placing it into my hands, she hugged
me. I kissed her face and hair, holding her tight.

The sound of chanting reached my ears and when I looked up, I saw the shaman and women entering the clearing. Seeing the look in my eyes, Maddie whispered something I will remember forever, "We all come from the stars, Mom." Tears flowed as I realized our time had ended, but I was grateful for the closure. I hugged her again and felt a heavy weight fall away. I know we will meet again.

"I love you, Madison Renee!"

Looking up with her impish grin, my daughter replied, "Love you, too!"

The women now encircled us, and the singing chant became ethereal.

"Gotta go, Mom," Maddie said as she gently pulled from my arms. Diamonds of light surrounded her form as it became misty, rose to the heavens and vanished.

The chanting ended and the women faded into the jungle until only the shaman remained. Wiping the tears from my eyes, I placed the new pendant around my neck.

"Thank you," was all I could say.

On another earth in
another time

Transformation
by Casandra Nightengale
© 2015

Journal Entry: *I am so very tired. Who could have imagined the speed with which the transformation has overtaken the people, especially the children? Some are adjusting well, taking it in stride, while others are not doing as well.   I am at a loss as to how to help them cope. I am a teacher, a mentor and guide for our precious next generation, yet, I am now expected to guide those who have already or are transforming; expected to have answers I do not possess. There is no need to be frightened, but the general population is not merely afraid, they are paranoid that they or, worse, their child may be the next to transform.*

It is genetic, that much we are sure of, but since we all spring from the same base stock, no one is exempt. And why should they be? The transformation is a gift as far as I am concerned--a releasing of what has been dormant for generations. But it is change and people resist change with a vengeance.

I need sleep.

With a deep sigh, Moria placed her pen on the desk and closed her journal. Leaning forward on her elbows, she placed her head into her hands, massaged her aching temples and then drew slender fingers through her shoulder length blond hair.

The Watchers had known for years that energies had been fluxing through the portals that surrounded their new world, but had not been concerned, even when a massive surge had coursed through the northern gate a year ago. Now people were changing.

Wearily, Moria once again scanned the energy readouts. Something niggled in a far corner of her brain, but exhaustion prevented it from entering consciousness. Finally, giving into her body's need for restorative sleep, she released the charts, teleported to her bed and was asleep in an instant.

Journal entry: *Eight days have passed since I last recorded my thoughts on the transformations. The Watchers say the energy is now pouring through more than one portal. Our people are becoming even more anxious. Fear is*

*also evident but, so far, violence has not broken
out.*

*Many of the children are now teleporting,
winking out and reappearing in an instant. They
are amused that they can do this. What is
startling to their elders is that they can
actually—in the blink of an eye—teleport to the
islands on the far side of the planet, and then
bring back indigenous flowers as proof that they
have been there. Rarely do our expert pilots risk
sending probes to those exotic islands, but the
band of severe vortex winds and deadly
lightning ringing the area do not seem to affect
the children at all.*

*A few of the adults who are changing—
including myself—can teleport, but our range is
not as extensive as the young ones. None of us
can, as of yet, reach the islands.*

"Moria, look," called a young voice.
Glancing up from her journal, Moria took in a
sharp startled breath. Her eight-year-old niece
sat in a full lotus position, her slender body
hovering four feet above the ground.

"Very good, Radnya. When did you
discover you could do that?"

"When I woke up this morning, I was floating above my bed," the child answered, a shy smile on her Elvin face. "Shaya can do it, too. He says we don't have to walk any more. We can float or fly or think ourselves to where we want to go, but I think it scares Gran-ma and Gran-da. When they think we are asleep, they talk about how bad times have come to our world. But you and Ma-ma say it's OK to be different. It isn't bad, is it? We didn't ask for the changes."

"Come here, Sweetie," Moria urged her niece. The girl flowed over into her outstretched arms. "Does it feel bad to do what you do?"

"No, but what is happening?"

"I don't know, Radnya, but you and your brother and all of the people who are changing are going to be OK," she reassured. "The science council is researching as much as they can and I'm sure they'll come up with an answer soon." Giving the child a hug, she added, "In the mean time, enjoy!"

Radnya grinned and teleported away.

School classes had been discontinued. It was impossible to keep students confined to desk and walls when they could levitate, teleport, and walk through solid objects. So the children played and experimented with their new abilities while the adults studied and researched.

One group of scientists discovered a repeating pattern to the energy pulses that now continually bombarded the planet and suggested that it was a message—that someone or something was trying to communicate with them. Others scoffed at the idea and countered that nothing on <u>their</u> sensors indicated anything sentient in the energy.

Meanwhile—people changed. Some doctors began to see dis-ease inside their patients and to cure them with a touch. Murky auras clued other lawgivers to untruths in witness testimony. Telepathy became common among the changed.

<u>Journal entry</u>: *Lately I have been having feelings of bi-location. My physical self can be sitting, reading, even teleporting, but another part of me seems to join the energy, to journey*

*to the portals, to bask in the never-ending
stream of light. I have sensed others there, too.
The scientists are right—someone is trying to
communicate with us. If we could only bridge
the gap that still remains, I feel the message
would become clear.*

"Moria, come quick! They are attacking
and I can't find Radnya and Shaya."

"Who are attacking?" Moria questioned
her sister, Korella.

"The militant dissidents, the ones who are
anti-change. They've liberated energy weapons
from the old colony ship and are marching on
the science complex!"

Together, the sisters teleported to the
scene.

Anger and fear were palpable radiations
from the militants now armed with stolen
weapons. Deadly, high-energy weapons that had
supposedly been destroyed once the newly
colonized planet had been deemed safe for
human life. The group was determined to take
over the science complex—to force the
scientists to reverse the change or to face fatal
consequences.

Then the children arrived, dozens of them—including Radnya and Shaya—teleporting between the militants and their target, hovering above the ground, smiling.

A keening whine filled the air as the energy weapons powered to full strength.

Knowing their peacekeepers had nothing that could withstand such an assault, parents, grandparents and even single adults attacked the dissidents only to be repelled by some sort of invisible force field that flung them back. Even those who could teleport could not penetrate its strength. In horror they watched, helpless, as the weapons were fired again and again. When the blinding brilliance subsided, they were astonished. The children were unharmed.

As the militants raised their weapons to fire another barrage, Radnya joined hands with her twin. All of the children linked hands. The force field became visible and wrapped itself around the dissidents, encasing them in a translucent globe of light before winking out.

When the children grinned, the adults knew that the globe—with its human contents—

was now on the far side of the planet. The weapons clattered harmlessly to the ground, flared brightly and vaporized.

While the crowd cheered, the children drifted to the ground.

"That was incredible!" Moria commented as she and Korella hugged the children later that night. "How did you stay safe?"

"Light bodies!" Shaya answered.

"Light bodies?" his mother queried.

"Of course," Moria answered. "Our light bodies are pure energy and can't be harmed by other energy! How clever of you to think of it."

"We didn't. They did," Radnya stated bluntly.

"They? Who are you talking about?" Korella asked.

"The portal beings. They told us how to shift to our light bodies. It tickles." Radnya giggled. Moria and Korella looked at each other.

"How do you communicate with these beings?" Moria asked.

"Just listen," Shaya sighed. To his sister, he added under his breath, "Grown-ups" as he rolled his eyes. Turning to his aunt, he continued, "They've been sending a message, but most people just don't listen. Here, let us help."

Shaya held Moria's hand and Radnya held Korella's. When the twins linked, light flooded the room and Moria again had the sense of bi-location. As the connection grew stronger, the message became clear.

"We are the portals through which the light of blessing flows to humankind. It is time to return to your true selves. Rejoice and be at peace."

About the Author:

Casandra Nightengale says her stories just appear and demand to be written. Some come from dreams or meditations. Others arrive while walking through the forests or looking out over the ocean in her beloved Pacific Northwest. In all cases, she sees them like a movie and tries to capture their essence.   She has recently relocated to Southwest Kansas for her health and to be close to friends and family. When she isn't writing, Casandra enjoys reading (complete with purring cat on lap), traveling, and photography. She may be contacted at: casandranightengale@gmail.com